I0420512

Crown
Everyday Coloring Book For Success Volume 4

Published by Kenneth Randal in 2015
First edition: First printing
Illustrations and design © 2015 Kenneth Randal
All rights reserved. No part of this book may be reproduced or transmitted in any form or by any means, including but not limited to information storage and retrieval systems, electronic, mechanical, photocopy, recording, etc. without written permission from the copyright holder.

ISBN-13: 978-1518701184
ISBN-10: 1518701183

www.ingramcontent.com/pod-product-compliance
Lightning Source LLC
Chambersburg PA
CBHW081150280526

45787CB00008B/3281